One Shade The More, One Ray The Less

A Poetry Compilation

Written & Illustrated by
Aayan Mulla

One Shade The More, One Ray The Less

Author: Aayan Mulla

Copyright © Aayan Mulla (2024)

The right of Aayan Mulla to be identified as author of this work has been asserted by the author in accordance with section 77 and 78 of the Copyright, Designs and Patents Act 1988.

First Published in 2024

ISBN 978-1-83538-325-4 (Paperback)
     978-1-83538-326-1 (E-Book)

Cover Design and Book Layout by:
    White Magic Studios
    www.whitemagicstudios.co.uk

Published by:
    Maple Publishers
    Fairbourne Drive, Atterbury,
    Milton Keynes,
    MK10 9RG, UK
    www.maplepublishers.com

A CIP catalogue record for this title is available from the British Library.

All rights reserved. No part of this book may be reproduced or translated by any form or by any means, electronic or mechanical, including photocopying, recording or by any information storage and retrieval system without written permission from the author.

The views expressed in this work are solely those of the author and do not necessarily reflect the views of the publisher, and the publisher hereby disclaims any responsibility for them.

To my grandma, Bibi Batool Rozindar!

My heritage of writing comes from you, as you published your poetry and life lessons in the form of stories, in newspapers and notable Indian periodicals. This inspired me to share my own words.

My journey began in early childhood, fueled by your belief in me. I wish you could see this moment—I know you would have cheered me on every step of the way.

Thank you for being my motivation and guiding light as I share my first collection of poems, "One Shade The More, One Ray The Less".

ACKNOWLEDGMENTS

I would like to thank Maple Publishing for guiding me and helping me throughout this journey. Without the constant guidance and support, compiling and completing this book would not have been possible.

Also, I would like to thank my parents, whose unwavering love and encouragement have been my greatest support.

CONTENTS

1. ACKNOWLEDGMENTS 4
2. Night Of Fire – Ottomans vs Vlad III 10
3. The Old Cottage 11
4. Chilli Jam 11
5. Christmas Eve 12
6. New Year's Fireworks 13
7. Train 14
8. Dunkirk 15
9. Jalebi 16
10. Biryani 17
11. Tringford Reservoir 18
12. Rose 19
13. Snowfall 20
14. Cherry Blossom 21
15. An Owl At Night 21
16. The Pear Tree 22
17. The Waterfall 23
18. Daffodils 24

19.	The Butterfly	24
20.	Moonlight	25
21.	Cherry Blossom	25
22.	The Rising Sun	26
23.	A Pomegranate	27
24.	Saffron	28
25.	Lotus	28
26.	Foxes In The Garden	29
27.	Parents	29
28.	The Indulgence Of A Fig	30
29.	Eagle	31
30.	Request To The Wren	32
31.	Sunset	32
32.	Sunset – Day 2	33
33.	Fireflies	33
34.	Pomegranate Again	34
35.	A Comet	34
36.	Blueberries	35
37.	Making Tea	35
38.	Fantasia Poetica	36
39.	Surreal	37

40.	Metamorphosis	38
41.	A Rose	38
42.	Blue Jay	39
43.	Dystopia	39
44.	White Cliffs	40
45.	The Phoenix	41
46.	An Ode To Shakespeare	43
47.	The Sirens	44
48.	Blue Eyes	45
49.	I Wish I Could	46
50.	K.P.	47
51.	The Fall Of Icarus	48
52.	Chrysaor	49
53.	The Tale Of Medusa	50
54.	Pegasus	51
55.	Hypnos	53
56.	Age	54
57.	Painting	54
58.	Identity	55
59.	Reflection	55
60.	Thread Of Fate	56

61.	Nature Of Reality	57
62.	Tranquil Chaos	57
63.	Fragments Of Dreams	58
64.	Refuge Of Illusion	59
65.	Das Mädchen	60
66.	Experience	61
67.	Much Ado About Nothing	63
68.	Pearls Of Wisdom	64
69.	Das Mädchen	65
70.	Hikikomori	66
71.	Mirror	70
72.	Triptych titled "Frozen in stone"	71
	1. Stone cold	71
	2. Nostalgia	73
	3. Tapestry	75
73.	Onde	76
74.	Scouring	77
75.	Faith	79
76.	Iron Maiden	80
77.	Autumn	81
78.	Scribe	82

79.	Faith	83
80.	Seasons	83
81.	TKAM	83
82.	M.L	84
83.	My Shadow	85
84.	Sepia	87
85.	Iris	89
86.	Oh Christmas Tree	90
87.	Ephemera	92
88.	Chiaroscuro	93
89.	Sanctum	94
90.	Medusa	95
91.	Butterfly	96
92.	Grapefruit	96
93.	Skull	97
94.	Onion	98
95.	Stylo plume	99
96.	Ethereal	100
97.	Sisyphus	101
98.	About The Author	102
99.	For the readers	103

Aayan Mulla

Night Of Fire – Ottomans vs Vlad III

Moonlight dances on the silky tents,
Quiet
Alarm!
Whistle of arrows beckon Death.
Soldiers pile every inch of Wallachian soil,
Clash metal
Silky, swords softly
Strike Death in its marble heart.
Ravaged Land.
Burnt tents.
Destruction.
Paranoia.
Terror.

One Shade The More, One Ray The Less

The Old Cottage

Cobwebs dance in wind,
Whispers resonate, listen,
Heart breaks into shards.

Chilli Jam

The world asunder,
A battle of sweet and spice,
Evokes ardent awe.

Aayan Mulla

Christmas Eve

Hark! Dost thou heareth the bells ringeth?
The snow-white angels carols singeth,
For today is Christmas eve,
The silvery light of the moon o'er trees,
The coniferous, gargantuan Christmas tree,
The metallic tinsel and vibrant wreaths,
The children's chortle and sharp glee,
The Christmas décor and floral leaves.
The sky turns from crimson to cerulean blue,
The red and white stockings are hung,
The sky shifts to a vermillion- a hazy hue,
Some could still hear the carols being sung.

One Shade The More, One Ray The Less

New Year's Fireworks

The countdown starts echoing through the sonorous bell,
My ears start ringing like a calcareous empty shell,
The frantic, rousing, raucous and unabating hoots,
The Eye took on a lustrous golden gleam,
Some may think it would be a riot it seems,
Many a people want to see this 'Tis a captivating desire,
The extravagant golden works of fire,
'Tis flamboyant and opulent 'neath the London Eye,
From far and near millions gaze, speculate and admire,
A splendorous blossom of pink and green nigh,
They disappear in many a momentous second,
After it, an assortment filled the noir as if beckoned,
The incessant, continual and reverberative din,
The hoots and uproarious cheers continued therein.

Aayan Mulla

Train

Red embers fill the sky,
The gears constantly turning,
Alerting people passing by,
The sun: red, hot, and burning.

From the railway carriage I see,
Grass, weeds, and ditches,
An azure sky and lots of trees,
A garden gnome and 12 witches.

Fields of corn and wheat,
A muddy stream flowing,
Disappear like haze and sleet,
Like dancing fireflies glowing.

The lush green meadows,
Amidst white and brown cattle,
The clouds casting shadows,
Like troops charging into battle.

One Shade The More, One Ray The Less

Dunkirk

Blood, trickling, lands
Unto shore. Sandy,
Agonizing screams;
Silently bled ears.
Strife and regret of life.
Heart of shards
Destroys you within. Conscience,
Faith, shrouded in despair.

Lands trickling blood
Sandy. Shore Unto
;screams Agonizing
Ears. bled Silently
Life of regret and Strife;
Within you Destroys
Shards of heart Conscience.
despair in shrouded ,Faith

Aayan Mulla

Jalebi

Spirals of heavenly ambrosia swirl,
As a millennia of tastes unfurl,
The crunchy saccharine coating,
One is in eternal Elysian, floating,
Inwards the noble nectar is spreading like sweet fire,
Filling one with sparks of ecstasy and spreading fragrance of fleur
Flakes of blanched almonds and pistachio green,
Scented oriental saffron sprinkled - threads of fire serene.

One Shade The More, One Ray The Less

Biryani

A mixture of spiced meat and rice,
Within it flowers of flavor and color,
It encompasses tastes and a millennium of spice,
The mesmerizing mint and oblivious onion,
Releasing flurries of richness from within,
An array of sweet, spicy spices from therein,
Creating enigmas of emotion from the heart,
A fusion of tastes from sweet to spicy waiting to depart,
The tender tasteful meat marinated with love and care,
The taste of exotic spices from cardamom to aniseed,
Flourishing like fresh, farm harvest grain,
A mixture of spiced meat and rice,
Within it flowers of flavor and color.

Aayan Mulla

Tringford Reservoir

The cloudless clear and azure sky,
Cacophonous as the seagulls' cry.
The shimmering and translucent lake,
Home to the brown mallard and drake.

The golden sun casts a scintillating glow,
On the sapphire blue waters below.
The hum and drum of boats and ships
And the smell of delicious fish and chips.

The great field of fresh pasture green
And the crisp and frigid air - clean;
The incessant barking of an aggressive dog
And the putrid smell of the unpleasant bog.

The ancient and rigid gargantuan trees
And the black ducks and chattering geese -
The serene, tranquil, and placid atmosphere
Heaven on Earth is nowhere, but here.

One Shade The More, One Ray The Less

Rose

The intricate, exquisite, silk petals,
Of the incarnadine and crimson rose
'Twas blooming with demeanor, aplomb,
In the lush, foliage with green boughs.

Many an incisive and perspicacious thorn,
Guards the grand and gracious flower.
The birds come singing every morn,
From far away to speculate and admire.

The rose has a place in history - near and afar,
From Blake's rose of affection and endearment.
To Shakespeare's rose of bloodshed and war -
The rose is special for its physiology and scent.

Aayan Mulla

Snowfall

Dancing
in
the
gale
A thousand pieces of stars;
Soft snow falls glittering yet pale.
The wind whistles away.

'Tis candy-colored, stained
With many a conflagration scent.
But woe, for it not remained
Pure and fresh, heaven sent.

Disappearing as dew in the sand,
Unto a flower and face
Cold to touch, but soft in hand.
'Twas a myriad of gems afloat.

One Shade The More, One Ray The Less

Cherry Blossom

The white petals of the thin trees,
Twirl around in the stormy breeze,
Through schools, plains, and meadows,
Casting humongous noir shadows.

An Owl At Night

The night sky sparkles;
An owl flutters to and fro
Craving attention.

Aayan Mulla

The Pear Tree

Oh, picturesque, prodigious pear tree,
Thou art an epitome of patience and peace,
Thou givest silky shade and fine pears as far as the eye can see,
And would continue to be so 'til you cease.
Thou givest many a luscious, russet, prickly pear,
Filled with appealing ambrosia and nectar,
Thine fruit hast no blemishes, it is fragile, fair.
Oh, picturesque, prodigious pear tree.

One Shade The More, One Ray The Less

The Waterfall

Dark blue, translucent, and flowing,
From the ice capped mountains and cliffs,
Cold icy freezing winds blowing.
As the gigantic ice glacier drifts, water
Eroding mighty rocks in its way,
Like a crazed and devastated thing,
'Tis an unstoppable force people say.
For its hunger is never satiated,
Hark! The water flowing down jagged rocks,
Come hither, for the sunshine awaits -
To see this paradisiacal wonder of the land.

Aayan Mulla

Daffodils

Dancing in the gregarious gale,
O'er high mountains and vale,
Are a group of daffodils yellow,
Making merry and mellow.

The Butterfly

Glass wings fluttered by
Through grassy knolls blossoms - hope
Like leaves in Autumn.

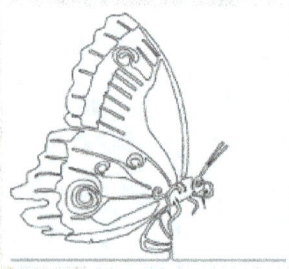

One Shade The More, One Ray The Less

Moonlight

The glimmering shine of the moon - glowing,
Silvery light o'er tree,
The wind near the dusky waters blowing,
A light and jaunty breeze.

Cherry Blossom

Pink and white showers,
The bough casts silky shadows,
Majestic wonder.

Aayan Mulla

The Rising Sun

From the picturesque, rugged, alpine mountain,
To the placid sparkling silky royal blue sea,
I see the sun rising - 'tis a glimmering fountain
Of halcyon, radiance and mellow are ye.
The melodious flowing of a deep blue waterfall,
Hark! The chirps of sparrows and the humble wren,
The radiant, majestic sunrise has now begun.
Ascending 'bove valleys scattered and glen,
The pure, overwhelming, and frigid clime,
The distant bells of silvery wind chime.
The myriads of bird seamlessly flow,
Looking down on the wonder below,
The sunrise will now costively end,
The magenta hue from clouds will transcend.

One Shade The More, One Ray The Less

A Pomegranate

The orchards of lush green bough,
The epicarp is ruby-red and shines like pearls,
Millions in a treasure chest here and now,
When you cut it open a world unfurls.
The jewels scatter in the scintillating sun,
Spreading ruby radiant illumination,
The world anew has begun,
The pinnacle of creation.
When you hold it betwixt your fingers,
The bitter blood stains your hands,
The guilt residing within lingers,
An act of heinousness in land.
The essence of jasmine and rose,
The beauty of orchids and lively lily,
Makes a heart content and grants repose,
Like still water - still and chilly.

Aayan Mulla

Saffron

Threads of golden fire,
Bursting with heartfelt desire,
Flavors fade like leaves.

Lotus

Cyclical Rebirth,
Pink flames lick muddy water,
Bounties - grace, beauty.

One Shade The More, One Ray The Less

Foxes In The Garden

Paw prints - spectral snow,
First rays of sunshine sparkle,
Foxes flit to fro.

Parents

Closest to my heart,
Embodiment of my hope,
A comet in the sky.

Aayan Mulla

The Indulgence Of A Fig

A fig loosely hangs,
    To a thick branch,
        Another fig,
           Dances in the wind.
The purple, brown skin,
Peels open and within it is reddish goodness,
    The fleshy mixture of pink,
    Is like sticky toffee.
Sticking to the roof of my mouth,
The sweet ambrosia flows through me and becomes part of me;
Another fig sways on a branch.
But it is green. I will wait for it...
For its skin to be rusty and peeling away like paint from an old room,
To harbor salvation.

And then I devour it.

One Shade The More, One Ray The Less

Eagle

The gilded bird was soaring,
In many serene azures skies,
The wet, wild wind is roaring,
He is the best of famous spies,
The razor-sharp hooked beak,
The plumage of golden and brown,
Cutting through skies grey and bleak,
He had ascended over cities and town,
The high and solitary eyrie,
In a cloudy night, dreary,
The brilliant starry skies above,
He, an intrepid beast returned to amongst foxgloves,
He is the king, he is regal,
None other than an eagle.

Aayan Mulla

Request To The Wren

Wren sing softly please,
You will awaken Slumber,
Shhh!!!

Sunset

A new beginning
Or is it so, casting remnants light on shadows
Slowly the glimmer fades into
Nothing

One Shade The More, One Ray The Less

Sunset – Day 2

The day has come to an end
      The success stays with you
The failures change into something better
      But the day is gone.

Fireflies

Fireflies glow softly,
Radiance flits across boughs,
Streaks light, sea of dark.

Aayan Mulla

Pomegranate Again

A globe of rubies,
Inside is there bitter blood,
Of the injured soul.

A Comet

Flash in starry sky,
A signal from the heavens,
An icy fire.

One Shade The More, One Ray The Less

Blueberries

Shards of azure infuse into the globule,
Frail skin like tissue paper,
Reveries of sweet and bitter,
Feel the blueberry go down your throat.

Making Tea

The water boiling,
Rustle of fragrant tea leaves,
Black ink stains water.

Aayan Mulla

Fantasia Poetica

Beautiful palaces decorated with rubies and pearl,
The violent waves crash o'er the rocks and whirl,
Chirps of the sparrow, cuckoo, and humble wren,
'Bove are cotton clouds, lush vales, and glorious glen,
Raised thrones studded with emeralds, made of damask and silk,
To eat ambrosia and drink sweet saffron nectar milk.

Surreal

Rose petals whisper dryly in the wind. Of longing. Of Hope. The sea softly strikes with its sword of spite taking away my treasures of silence. I gaze at my reflection on the waters of Fire. Gold granules rush through my feet. Unaware. Of what lay ahead. The Day ascends the steps of Night, staining the shards of azure mosaic with streaks of rose gold, beckoning it to end. Day stains the canvas with ink, allowing night to take charge. He snaps his fingers to awaken the soldiers of the sky - stars to guard the Night, his general the Moon shows herself to the world. Grace, Beauty, and Virtue dance till the streaks of a wounded god's blood awaken ignorant Humanity.

Aayan Mulla

Metamorphosis

Slimy striking creature of jade,
Is prisoner in the wraps of smooth silk,
Frozen in time like a fossil,
Emerges as a silvery sapphire butterfly.

A Rose

Papier mâché petals,
Stained with the deep ink of life,
Glide gently on soil.

One Shade The More, One Ray The Less

Blue Jay

Silky snow orator spies,
Inky feathers cut through day,
Sea embroidered in his plumage,
Each feather stained of sin

Dystopia

Embers of hope flit,
Dystopia's icy grip,
Behemoths in charge.

Aayan Mulla

White Cliffs

Ashen clouds foxtrot,
In
The sea of blue,
Of birds,
Crisp air,
Tears the clouds asunder,
Gleaming like the Great Pyramids,
In the scintillating Shine of die Sonne,
Silky sea flutters,
Like the flag of a 3rd World country,
Horns of ships and cruises,
Remind you of the human world,
Grassy knolls wave,
Like daffodils on a meadow,
Deafening sirens awaken,
You for yet another day.

One Shade The More, One Ray The Less

The Phoenix

Rising from its ashes starting anew
A glowing star descended and grew
Into a majestic and miraculous bird
Never seen by any or heard
The glowing bird of fire
Soared in the skies polluted and dire

Like a jewel emitting a radiance of light
The phoenix was soaring in the darkness of the night
Spreading shreds of knowledge on its path
And ending every heinous monster's wrath
Enlightenment was finally found
The knowledge of it is very profound

Made of smokeless fire that burns many
The phoenix never hurt any

Aayan Mulla

Example of life it was
Helping humanity for a greater cause
The epitome of rebirth it was
Teaching humanity the Creator's laws
Appreciating the goodness and reforming the flaws

The tale of the Phoenix does not end here

One Shade The More, One Ray The Less

An Ode To Shakespeare

'Shall I compare thee to a summer day?'
The scintillating sun and freshly cut hay,
Thou art from the beginning a wonder,
Creating a world from one, torn asunder,
From the sumptuous green world,
As the chaos in Verona unfurled,
Delphic lines are carved and engraved,
Unto thine epitaph and grave.

Aayan Mulla

The Sirens

The cerulean briny waves are churning,
O'er sparkling shores and golden sands,
The sun is flaring blazing and burning,
Near is verdant and halcyon land,
Waves of harmony and choral melodies,
Wafted towards us like the famed Pan's flute,
The legend spread in the imperial seven seas,
Akin to Apollo's illustrious necked lute: 'Come nigh o sailors of the ship'
The alluring voices would incessantly chant,
For a sporadic phenomenon was to come - an eclipse,
Ears stuffed with beeswax, my comrades and I,
Would dare not to veer close by.

One Shade The More, One Ray The Less

Blue Eyes

The brilliant sapphire blue eyes,
Are a briny, adriatic and capacious sea,
Time instantaneously flies
I see an angelic figure- thee,

I feel serenity and quietude,
My heart feels like a Formula 1,
I see them in the sky- solitude,
The waves, crashing against a rocky shore.

I see them in the tumultuous sea,
Sights I have never seen before,
I see an ethereal being -thee.

The majestic sunrise in the glen,
The chirp of the birds at dawn,
Take me to where it all began,
Do not leave me forlorn.

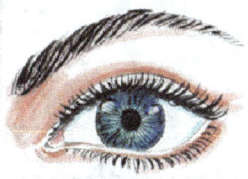

Aayan Mulla

I Wish I Could...

I wish I could live in an amicable world,
Where words did not hurt more than spears being hurled,

I wish I could live in a world-serene,
In which were wonderous sceneries unfurled-empyrean.

I wish I could stop the conflicts of many a warring nation,
And eradicate vagrancy by stopping inflation,

I wish I could reduce nations stricken by poverty,
By giving them resources to spend at their liberty,

I wish I could give every child an education,
To help them achieve their full potential,

I wish I could make people embrace equality as a whole,
Between race, religion, and many a gender role,

I wish I could live in an amicable world,
Where words did not hurt more than spears being hurled.

One Shade The More, One Ray The Less

K.P

Thou hath lips redder than rose,
Thou art more elegant than poetry or prose,
Thou hast teeth whiter than pearl,
Within thou doth beauty unfurl,
The radiant moon envies thine face,
Thou art an epitome of true Grace,
Thine cheeks hath a scarlet hue,
Thine eyes art a silky sea blue,
Thou hath luxuriant brown tresses,
Thou art a star in the sea of dark,
Thou hath a voice choral'st lark,
Thou art a brilliant meteor that goes,
Thou hath lips redder than rose,
Thou art more elegant than poetry or prose.

Aayan Mulla

The Fall Of Icarus

Glued with wax, a multitude of widespread wings,
Rested on the back of the ill-fated Icarus,
For he glided as smoothly as harp strings,
Struck in the heart by Ignorance,
The gusts, sirening him to fly close to the Sun,
Alas! The disastrous damage had been done,
The wax began to melt in the sweltering heat,
One after another the feathers pulled away,
From eagles, magpies, owls, blackbirds, and goldfinches sweet,
The clouds began to huddle and darkened was the day,
There was a soft snowfall of many a color,
He was to die for his thirst to discover,
He clenched his fists in triumph as tears streaked across his countenance welcoming the cadence of the silky blue sea,
The silent current washed him of all feathers making him formless and free.

Chrysaor

Severed from lifeless body Medusa's head,
Forth sprung Chrysaor - a giant of a man,
His hands held a sword golden, mighty,
A symbol of patriarchy and feat of strength was he,
Later, he married Callirrhoe- one of the Oceanids,
Alongside which he became the King of Iberia,
Had he a son named Geryon - a three headed warrior killed by Heracles.

Aayan Mulla

The Tale Of Medusa

Daughter of the primordial gods of the sea,
She had the gift of beauty and grace,
She decided a priestess of Athena to be,
However, such an incident takes place, no longer does Athena wants to see her face,
In an act of utter coldness of the heart Athena punishes her by transforming her into a beast,
With bronze hands and wings and a venomous nest of snakes for hair,
From an apex being her favorite devotee, she now becomes the least.
Who would believe this was a maiden fair,
She is now given the power to turn any to stone,
But only if they look into her eyes,
Henceforth, was she left alone,
For if they had looked in her eyes, they would have found betrayal and lies,
Throughout history is she a cautionary tale,
Of blind faith leading to no avail.

One Shade The More, One Ray The Less

Pegasus

The exceptional equine with wings and a pure heart,
Son of Medusa and Poseidon is the winged steed,
He to Mount Helicon was ready to depart,
This was the abode of the Muses where he arrived with speed.
Hitting the ground with his hoof many a time,
And lo! materializes the Hippocrene spring,
The one who water from it drank would compose music and rhyme,
And would creative instillation in oneself bring.

Tamed was he with the grand golden lace,
With the help of Athena, goddess of wisdom and war,
Obliterated he Chimera of the Earth's face,
The monster ravaging the kingdom of Lycia afar.

When Bellerophon tried to reach the Olympus mount,
A horsefly bit Pegasus, throwing his rider down,
Bellerophon fell thousands of feet losing count
Spent his days Bellerophon, blind and lame in a distant town.

Aayan Mulla

Decided Zeus the deities' king,

To turn Pegasus into a constellation of many a glimmering star,

Soon was Pegasus a symbol of many creative and poetic thing,

And his heroic tale was spread afar.

One Shade The More, One Ray The Less

Hypnos

Son of Darkness and the Night,
On the entrance of thine cave grow flowers bright,
Thou sleepest on an ebony bed,
Near thine grotto grow poppies red,
From thine abode comes river Lethe,
Where Night and Day meet.

Aayan Mulla

Age

A reflection paints the canvas of water,
Innocence in human form,
Age casts its spell and wrinkles,
Stretches and the face distorted.

Painting

Brush rustles in paint,
Creates plethora of strokes,
Splashes of color.

Identity

My reflection in front of me,
Is the exact same,
But the most different,
Who am I?

Reflection

A battle of thoughts,
A being crossed paradigm,
Possibilities.

Aayan Mulla

Thread Of Fate

A piece of thread,
Dances in my hands,
Intertwines and straightens,
A knot can be many things:
Kinship. Betrayal. Heartbreak.
But when it is severed,
Emotions are murdered.

One Shade The More, One Ray The Less

Nature Of Reality

Intricate and geometric china plate,
Splashes of cyan and splatters of red,
Harbors a reflection of silver fangs,
And pale skin with blood eyes.

Tranquil Chaos

Tranquility smiles,
Cacophony of footsteps,
Deafening their ears.

Aayan Mulla

Fragments Of Dreams

An intricate porcelain vase shatters,
Into a sea of shards,
You step on it,
Beads of blood stain the geometric tiles,
Tears streak your countenance,
Haze envelopes the scene,
You wake up shuddering,
Sleep clouds your eyes but you fight,
Lifting the dismal duvet,
You check your foot,
Scratch free.

One Shade The More, One Ray The Less

Refuge Of Illusion

Melting gold orb shines bright.
Casting glow in orange, purple skies.
Waterfalls flow cascading gently.
Across jagged granite twisting sharply
Rivers of wine, honey, and milk
Harmoniously furtively flow.
Magenta flamingos dance gracefully.
Pounding headache softly as sword,
Splintering rapturous reveries.
Shards of stellar imagination
Unmasks Illusion's facetious façade.
He lies shrunken near a wall
Damaged. Decay. Dying.
A dubious syringe
Jabbed in his arm. Barely breathing.
Nostrils flaring. Darkness begins his dance.
Nicotine-stained teeth rotting.
He smiled.

Aayan Mulla

Das Mädchen

The moon is your face,
Radiant in silky waters,
Your brilliant breath,
A symphony of roses and jasmine,
Eyes are a way to see the world,
But my world is you and,
Your eyes windows to your soul,

One Shade The More, One Ray The Less

Experience

Heart melts,
        Like candy floss,
                Into cotton.
Wisps of wind,
        Chiming slowly,
                It's return.
Soul snaps,
        In two halves,
                Rippling cross.
Heart melts,
        Like candy floss,
                Into cotton.

Unrequited Soul.

Flutters,
        Across
                Waterfalls Of Fire,
 Across
        Ravaged Lands,
                Of Blood.
Paints sky
        Color of souls.
                Bound in chains of hope,

Aayan Mulla

To find you.
      In rivers
                        Of hope,
    Embittered.

Valleys of silence,
      Reverberate,
                Unrequited.

One Shade The More, One Ray The Less

Much Ado About Nothing

A mockingbird,
Rising through Elizabethan clouds,
Of Despair and Death,
Trial Of Fire awaits. Hero,
Wars of words: hurtful, bitter,
Stabbed in the back,
With the Dagger of Betrayal,
Honor tainted
With Blood,
Bound in chains
Of Patriarchy.
She dies,
Only to live again.

Aayan Mulla

Pearls Of Wisdom

Arrogance and Wisdom are like
The bee and the flower,
Moonlight gently gleaming
On the Pearls of Wisdom.

Arrogance hides in shards of shadow;
The leaves are fluttering, in pain
But shatters against the light of wisdom,
Vanquished by Wisdom's nobility.

No amount of arrogance will tarnish the seed;
This is the seed that was harvested, now the tree bears fruit,
Which will not be fruits of despair and darkness,
But the fruits of kindness and humility.

One Shade The More, One Ray The Less

Das Mädchen

Your eyes are a sea, gleaming like a dagger;
Your blonde tresses are like honey floss
You plague my dreams:
Dreams of tranquility in the vast empyrean
Your face like a porcelain mask.
Love is blind, but not deaf.
But you are the dream of my heart.
You slowly depart
With me in the gardens of Life,
And we will sit under the tree of Hope
Flowers in the garden of the heart, their beauty is unmatched
Imagining what life would have
Been if we had stopped dreaming
Dreams give Hope wings
Only to come again
Would our hearts have changed?
Or our thinking?
Goodbye,
In every beat of my heart, your name is engraved.

Aayan Mulla

Hikikomori

I

Pastel de Nata
        Crumbs
                Coat
                      My leather sofa
2-1
        Spain wins 2024 Euros.
That does not matter
                Shut from society
Rain pours on
                And on.
Going at 50mph
        Listening to a vague song

The bed is comfortable,
Oh look!
            A deer's carcass
                And my Conscience
            Stained with its innocence
In the moonlight
        Grand piano
                      Hallways
        Espresso shots

One Shade The More, One Ray The Less

                      End of years results.
In every beat of my heart, your name is engraved.
Is that what Sherlock told
                Victoria when he
Punctured his wall with bullet holes?
                VA

The rose gold MacBook
                Glitters in the nightlamp
Honeydew drips
                From my mouth
      Like mangoes,
           They are decayed
now
Stop.
      Listen to your heartbeat....
Reminding yourself,
        Existing
                "Vieni via con me"

Aayan Mulla

II

Gilded ceilings
                        Shine in the moonlight
      Reflecting upon ancient volumes
          Ivory paper
              Ages like Miss Havisham's wedding cake
                    To a yellow sky, but no sun
Dolce Vita on the rocks
Melted into a slimy puddle
          To snatched strife.
                    Meisterstück 149 Classique
Lying among strewn things,
              My things.
A torn brochure on
        Capri
        "Vieni a capri" in bold lettering
    Piano plays on,
My heart's plight and pain
My fond memories
                    Unwritten letters
        Stamped with a crimson wax insignia
              tied with brown string
Or should I say unposted?
    The envelopes
           Yellowed with age

One Shade The More, One Ray The Less

The ink dried with my tears.
Fountain strewn across the hall
                        Marble ashen like my bones
                Yet strong like my soul
The letters sliced neatly
            With a bronze penknife
Insignia broken into fragments,
      A nail struck through the heart of the letter
Splintering into rapturous
                Reveries and shards of sharp yet
                Stellar imagination
My life opened like
        Pastel de Nata
            Crumbs
                Coat
                        My leather sofa
                              "Vieni via con me"

Aayan Mulla

Mirror

Artists are free
Not bound by chains of realism
With their fountain pens and paintbrushes
Their reflection of life's stream
Its waves crashing over one another
Is through someone else
Something else
They are like the slivers of moon
Reflecting themselves through the sun
For if they write what they feel
What their empty heart desires
Their ashen shell-like persona
Will be broken like
Shards of mirror reflecting moonlight.

Triptych titled "Frozen in stone"

1. <u>Stone cold</u>

Yellow tents
    Flutter
        In the wind
They return
    Home
        To their
        dead

Malnourished
    Impoverished
        Abandoned
Onions
    Flow from
        Their eyes
Like
    Purple
        Amethyst
Betrayal
    Broken glass
        Barren

Layers of

Aayan Mulla
    Lilac
        Leftovers
Mothers
    Weeping
        Tears of blood
Fathers
    Cry silently
        At night
Children pray
    They were
        Anywhere else
They wake
    Not to the
        Chimes of an alarm clock
But to
    Showers
        Of golden bullets
As I read
    This article
        My eyes pricked
With onions
    My face solemn
        With a hint of
            familiarity

One Shade The More, One Ray The Less

2. **<u>Nostalgia</u>**

Made of night's skin.
                The stars melted in as   i n k.
                      Shadows void of sun

S
      I
          N
                G

      of their suffering.

Lilac flames with pine ash
empties

        into the valley
            reaching a scintillating
zenith.
      Seagulls float

      midair.

      Conifer trees whistle
            a distant name.
Buttons of gilded insignia

      Branded
            in ivory.

Aayan Mulla

Selene
                Yearns for
                              Endymion.
Marble psyche
            Forever turns
                        Stone
Like the
        Famed
                      Gorgon

My creative faculties
        Tired of
                      Fabricating it all
All my stories
        Poetry
                    Prose
Forged in flames
        of Expression's shadow

        From the abyss   Of my soul.

One Shade The More, One Ray The Less

3. **<u>Tapestry</u>**

Bone white
Birch shines   Eerily   In moonlight
Sky darkens   Clouds huddle   Whispering secrets
Sky stained   Blood red   Chained   By Hope
Wings of Shadow   Cut through the   Day from Time to time.
Mars plunges his sword   Deep into Our already warring world
All   people's   Hearts   Frozen. Stone cold.   Oblivious
My eyes   wearily   gaze at
my 100-word essay slowly
I change a few words,
fix a few errors   dissatisfied   press   SUBMIT

My words
ring true
We need
to try
Each day to
Strive
to change
The tapestry
of
Opinion.

Aayan Mulla

Onde

Swan of shadow
Floats across the Styx
Feathers of wet ink
Whistling a grasshopper's tune
Its path carving statues of stars.

One Shade The More, One Ray The Less

Scouring

Crack of nutmeg
Bitter yet woody, floral
People are rushing past
Not for a train to catch
Not for a football match
For something, a lot bigger
Huddle of footsteps
What kind of act did you do?
Yesterday,
10 years ago,
In your last moments.
Was it holding the door open?
Or was it a smile?
Or helping the old lady from across the hall?
Think.
For time is of the essence
Not the nutmeg you heard at the start
Something far more important
You are to stand with your honorable deeds
Some have mountains of them
And some have a speck of sand
In front of your creator,
Day of Reckoning is here

Aayan Mulla

You rush past someone you feel you know
Their face instigates a warm feeling in your stomach
Your eyes prick with tears, you do not know who they are
But it all just snaps
Like a bitter reverie, shards purging your soul of sin
If your deeds were the droplets of water in the sea,
You would yearn, give anything to go back
Do one more good deed
In exchange for anything.
Crack of nutmeg
Bitter yet woody, floral
People are rushing past
But now you know why.

One Shade The More, One Ray The Less

Faith

1. Were humans being stewards of the Earth?
2. What led to their downfall?
3. Were they eloquent in speech?
4. Was human life valued over materialistic paraphernalia
5. Were they a greedy people?
6. Who was their leader?

1. Climate change was eradicating the Earth's ozone layer and yet humans continued to have their way.
2. Their insolence and failure in the game of world diplomacy. Wronged by oppressors who were proud.
3. No, their words were spears of racism and classism which punctured the souls of the illiterate and impoverished.
4. No in fact human life was a currency used to spend trade to gain recognition on the world stage and international intrigue
5. Yes, they used each other for purposes unfit, to commit acts of bloodshed and tyranny. Brainwashed and barren until the only things they can do was follow orders from the higher ups.
6. Each continent (there were 7) had a separate leader who was "elected" by its people. Democracy became dictatorship and diplomacy became derided

Aayan Mulla

Iron Maiden

Citrus rind
                Reminiscing sun
                              Lilacs dance
In the Zephyr
              Sweet like
                          Tonka bean
Dissolve
              Into tapestries of shadow
                          Eclipsed like
                          Eurycleia
       By a conch shell
                        Over moonlight
              Ubiquitous
        Selene yearns
                    For Endymion
        Like sea
                For salt
For
     All
                    Eternity
   To
        Come

One Shade The More, One Ray The Less

Autumn

                Ochre
   Leaves   Fall
Fluttering in   the   Zephyr   of   life
  Skeletons   start to grow   leaves of
         sun   slowly
Shedding their scales like a serpent
Until the tattered skin falls like ochre
     Leaves   To   Reveal
        Beginning
           A
           G
           A
           I
           N

* Shape of a maple leaf

Aayan Mulla

Scribe

Quills
Scrape   On
Harsh   Animal   Skin
Until   Eternity
Ink
Splatters
Like
Sin

Staining
Tapestry of
Conscience

* Shape of a key

One Shade The More, One Ray The Less

Faith

Dreams are where humans can traverse
Regardless of worldly qualifications or achievements
Across borders and land and sea uncharted
Only holding on to the rope one calls faith

Seasons

Daffodils are blooming
Soaking in the summer sun
The soil riddled with maple leaves
Lying underneath a sheet of snow

TKAM

Innocence - murdered,
Disparity - dark and light,
Biased is Justice.

Aayan Mulla

M.L

Sfumato makes you real.
Yet the gilded frame makes you fictional
Why is that?
Am I real?
Those eyes, are they sad?
Or happy
Sad because of millions crowding around you,
Lack of personal space
Or happy because of the attention.
What dress is that?
Silk, your husband's gift.
The natural beauty, the frigid air, enjoying it?
Or just a place of retreat?
Stop following me across the room.
Please.

*M.L is Mona Lisa

My Shadow

My shadow always sticks to me
All the time chortling and gleeing
Like it was trying to flee
It was gliding over the trees
    My Shadow

My shadow always dresses up immaculate and neat
The speed at which it saunters
I can never beat
It always greets my parents
A 100 times nicer than me
And sometimes it has a mind of its own
Always being solitary and alone
I hate one thing and he loves it
One and only: Sleep
    My Shadow

I dont always need him by my side
But when I do need him, it vanishes
Into thin air, and it never shows
Up again which leaves me forlorn
    My Shadow

Aayan Mulla

My shadow has a need of sleep
It sometimes gives me the creeps
He acts a 100 times meeker than me
More sincere than me

    My Shadow

*Written in Year 6

One Shade The More, One Ray The Less

Sepia

Gold
     leaves
          Scatter
               everywhere
Fragile
     Like
          Dew
               drops
Lush
     Green
          Tree
              of
                 life
Is
     now
          skeleton
              ashen
                 white
Shadows
     dance
          Moon's
              aura
Sparkles

Aayan Mulla

      distant
           seas
Winds
      whisper
               a
                      distant
                          name
Of
      Yearning

One Shade The More, One Ray The Less

Iris

Manilla Letters
Unposted correspondences
Stamped with crimson insignia
The bohemian ink a deep shade
Of iris
Hidden in a leather bounded
                                      Notebook
Selene yearns
                for Endymion
Her life a yellow sky without sun
Sweet yet powdery, the smell
Pervaded the room
Where I kept my secrets
All of them
Don't tell a
Soul.

Aayan Mulla

Oh Christmas Tree

Oh Chrismas Tree, Oh Christmas Tree
How much elation you make me feel
The gifts underneath you enjoying the
Shade and breeze

The carols and tree make the
Mood very Christmasy
The variety of ornaments that
Ornate you
On Christmas eve, the wind
Singing along

Oh Christmas Tree, Oh Christmas Tree
How much joy you make feel
The gifts underneath you enjoying the
Shade and breeze

All the houses with overpowering smells
Of stew roast potatoes greeting me
With joy
The luscious turkey wafting thorough
The wondrous wide windows

One Shade The More, One Ray The Less

Oh Chrismas Tree, Oh Christmas Tree
How much elation you make me feel
The gifts underneath you enjoying the
Shade and breeze

* Written in Year 6

Aayan Mulla

Ephemera

The mother of pearl moon cratered with briquettes
Time and tide wait for no man
I will be in a boat with a watch to that shall I say
The mother of pearl moon cratered with briquettes
I will be in a boat with a watch in the breezily frigid clime
The moon like a polished silver dime
The mother of pearl moon cratered with briquettes
Time and tide wait for no man

One Shade The More, One Ray The Less

Chiaroscuro

In the shadows and light
The wind whistles away
It was there throughout the night

Who am I
Wind whistles away
In the shadows and light

Who am I
The wind whistles away
It was there throughout the night

Who am I
The wind whistles away
In the shadow and light

Who am I
Wind whistles away
It was there throughout the night

Who am I
Wind whistles away
In the shadow and light
It was there throughout the night

Aayan Mulla

Sanctum

Azure skies
Blinded me
Halcyon radiance
Of the golden orb
Stung me
Waves lapping
beneath my feet

But someone might not
Be so lucky

Instead, they might say
Grey skies
Reflected my future
I was not fortunate enough
To get a ray of radiance
The only thing
                              beneath my feet
Is my shadow

One Shade The More, One Ray The Less

Medusa

Look in the mirror
Do not.
Long tresses are snarling snakes
Blue eyes are green pebbles
A spider crawls near a wall
I glimpse and
It
        d
        r
        o
        p
        s
    On the floor

Aayan Mulla

Butterfly

Flitting from corners of the sky
Leaves flutter in the light breeze
Mosaic tapestry shimmers by
Amongst woodland trees

Grapefruit

Outer coating of melting gold
Hues of amber, tales told
Of the humble grapefruit fair
Pink flesh shards bitter compare

One Shade The More, One Ray The Less

Skull

Charred bone skull slowly
Glistens in the dark night
I look at it. Stare at its empty eyes
I feel the thoughts it had
Or he. Or she. Or. Never mind
I imagine what its face would be like
Round, narrow or skeletal?
Its eyes – Blue or brown
My reverie splinters into
Shards of imagination
When I investigate it
I see possibilities

Aayan Mulla

Onion

Layers of grief, sadness, and pain
Send you to a trip down memory lane
You try to remember you really do
Alas! Nothing rings a bell, nothing true
Ah yes! You were in the kitchen near
All your fears were to disappear
You were chopping an onion brightly pink
Tsunamis of tears, no time to blink
It is the best at hiding secrets and lies
You traverse parallel worlds time flies
In a fit of rage, sublime
Time spins like a tornado but this time
You stab the onion in its heart
Looking down at the mutilated soul depart

One Shade The More, One Ray The Less

Stylo plume

Irreplaceable
Blood transfigures ink
Through thick and thin
Expresses your soul
For the better or worse

Aayan Mulla

Ethereal

In the forests of Transylvania.
Sea of dark chaos.
It lingers in the shadows.
Fangs of fury glinting.
In the mesmerizing moonlight.
Blood flows through its throat.
Coldly. Silent. Content.
It was electric.
"Come downstairs," Mom calls.
I look at my Halloween costume.
Thoughts battle in my mind.
But I rush downstairs. Ready.

One Shade The More, One Ray The Less

Sisyphus

Some days I wonder if my life would still be like this
The plight of it all
People think I am just rolling a boulder up a hill
But it is so much more than that
At this point it is not even the task.
The boulder just rolls back down again
I am not guilty of killing those travelers.
They stole from me.
I was the one who fed them, put a roof over their head
And yet they had the audacity to steal from me
So, I do not care if I will have to be doing this for eternity
People remember me in ridicule
But I am the greatest hero.
Greater than Hercules.

Aayan Mulla

ABOUT THE AUTHOR

Aayan Mulla is currently studying in a prestigious secondary school in London. He lives in Chigwell, UK with his parents.

He compiled his first poem at the age of 7. He is a voracious reader. His hobbies include creative writing, and poetry, enabling him to publish his work in school newsletters. He is also an active participant in various global poetry competitions.

His love of the written word stems from his heritage of writers, notably his late maternal grandmother, inspiring him to publish this compilation.

Through this book he hopes to enrich young peoples' minds towards poetry and their perspective.

You can reach the author on Instagram: at uk.aayan or email: uk.aayan@gmail.com

For the readers

Ballad – Conveys the narrative in a short and structured way. This was originally meant to be sung along with background music.

Example in the book – "The Tale of Medusa"

Calligram – A calligram is words arranged to form a picture. This is aesthetically pleasing and quite creative at the same time. Visual poetry evokes more response from the reader as they read something and see it at the same time.

Example in the book – "Tapestry" (third part of "Triptych")- A triptych is a three paneled piece of art and shows 3 scenes on each panel. They form a story. The title for the 3rd poem "Tapestry" is figurative as the shape is meant to represent a tree.

Free verse - A poem without a specific rhyme scheme, used to reflect continuous ideas like speech. Putting it into rhyme schemes distorts its meaning.

Example in this book – **"M.L"**- On the Mona Lisa in the Louvre. It captures her penetrating gaze and surreal smile but also what is behind it all.

Haiku - A poetic form originating in Japan traditionally following the 5-7-5 pattern where the first line consists of 5 syllables, the second consists of 7 syllables and lastly the third line returns to the 5-syllable structure at the start. However, it does not have to follow the 5-7-5 rule to be a haiku. Brevity in word choice matters.

Examples in this book – Non traditional haiku – "Fireflies" Traditional haiku – "The Old Cottage"

Interrogative poetry – The use of question and answer in poetry makes the reader more curious as to what will happen next. A famous example is "What were they like?" by Denise Levertov. It is presented through the lens of the Vietnam war.

Example in the book – "Faith"- This poem explores a post-apocalyptic world where humans are being questioned by a higher form of life.

Ode – A jubilant poem to celebrate someone special or has made lots of contributions.

Example in the book - "An ode to Shakespeare". This celebrates the most famous English playwright in the world, William Shakespeare.

Palindrome – A palindrome is something the same read forwards and backwards; for e.g., racecar or even phrases for e.g. "Do Geese see God" But for poetry this takes a lot of time and effort to ensure there is a different meaning each time if read from top to bottom and vice versa.

Example in the book – "Dunkirk"- Although not differing in meaning, it is an interesting take on war and conflict as it is continuous.

Quatrain - A poetic form which uses two rhyming couplets. The poem consists of 4 lines. Due to 2 alternating rhyming couplets being used, it has an ABAB rhyme scheme.

Example in the book - "Butterfly"- This quatrain illustrates the brevity of the butterfly through the use of evocative imagery while adhering to the structure.

Rhyming couplet – Two alternating lines of poetry that rhyme. This makes a poem more musical and gives it a meter (rhythmic structure of a line of poetry shown by stressed or unstressed syllables).

Example in the book – "The tale of Medusa"- This poem explores the Greek myth of Medusa, giving background about her past and her current state. It does not put her in a bad light but tries to see what is behind the woman with a head full of snakes.

Rhyme scheme – Pattern of rhyme at the end of a line in a poem. This enhances its meter and musicality. There are letters assigned to each line and if the alternate end of a sentence rhyme, it is known as an ABAB rhyme scheme.

Sestet – This is a poem consisting of 6 lines, not following the rhyme scheme.

Example in the book – Hypnos – The Greek god of Sleep's habitat is described in this poem.

Sonnet – A poem consisting of 14 lines. There can be a variety of rhyme schemes for this but the one that works best is the rhyming couplets, they have an ABAB rhyme scheme. Shakespeare would often use this rhyme scheme in his sonnets for e.g., "Shall I compare thee to a summer's day?"

Example in this book – "Tringford Reservoir"- This describes the beautiful reservoir on a sunny day.

Triolet - A poem of 8 lines in which the first, third and seventh line are repeated. The second and the eighth line are repeated. The third and fourth lines are rhyming and fifth and sixth are also rhyming.

Example in this book - "Ephemera" - Dreamlike and quite imaginative although quite difficult to write with its tight constraints.

Villanelle – A French sonnet consisting of 19 lines: The rhyme scheme is particularly challenging to explain.

Example in this book - "Chiaroscuro"

www.ingramcontent.com/pod-product-compliance
Lightning Source LLC
Chambersburg PA
CBHW071215070526
44584CB00019B/3043